# QUATRAINS

## OF

# KHALILULLAH
# KHALILI

The Octagon Press
London

Requests for permission to reprint, reproduce, etc. to:
Permissions Department, The Octagon Press Ltd.,
14 Baker Street, London W1M 1DA, England

ISBN 90086084 7

Printed and Bound in Great Britain by
Redwood Burn Limited
Trowbridge & Esher

تفضل العلامة الكبير والشاعر النابغة الاستاذ محمد بهجـة الأثري
فنقل هذه الرباعيات الى اللغة العربية نظماً • وسوف تنشر هــذه الترجمة
الشعرية الجديدة قريباً باذن الله •

\* \* \*

اقدم شكري الخالص الى صديقي الكاتب الفاضل الاستاذ مشكور
الاسدي واقدم امتناني القلبي العميق لمواطني الشاب الفاضل علي شريف
الافغاني لمساعيهما المشكورة في تدوين هذه المجموعة البسيطة •

خليـــلي

*Dedication*

Presented to my friend and fellow-countryman the great
*Arif*, Janab-i-Idries Ali Shah

Khalili
1977

## Introduction

### By Professor Khalilullah Khalili

This collection of my *Ruba'iyat*, Quatrains, has been published three times in my beloved country, Afghanistan, twice in Iran, and again in Baghdad, Iraq, in a trilingual Edition.

My sincere thanks and gratitude to my dear compatriot and friend the *Arif* (Sufi Illuminate) The Sayed Idries Shah. Through his aid and encouragement, the work is now published in the United Kingdom.

Praise to Idries Ali Shah, who has written and published many precious books in varied fields of knowledge. Especially to be appreciated are his brilliant and important services in revealing the celestial inspirations and inner thoughts of the great teachers of Islam and Sufis: for the Children of Mankind are now more than ever in need of light and guidance in this society of today, where materialism increasingly preponderates over spirituality.

Khalili
19.3.1980.

*Translator's Note*


This English version of the forty Ruba'iyat (Quatrains) of the Afghani thinker and poet, Khalilullah Khalili, is based on the Arabic translation of the Persian original.

It might, perhaps, be of some interest to make a few remarks about these Ruba'iyat, by way of introduction.

To begin with, one is inevitably tempted to compare these verses with the Ruba'iyat of the illustrious poet of Nishabor, Omar Khayyam. Like his famous predecessor, Professor Khalili's scope is very wide and he covers in his own Ruba'iyat a variety of topics. These embody, above all, the poet's spiritual unrest in search of eternal truths, as well as his deep concern for the enigma of creation, life and death. They also present a fine satirical sense of the unreasonableness of human beings. In the Ruba'iyat, too, we can clearly discern Khalili's evident enjoyment of life, its pleasures and beauties. Indeed, in some of his verses, he comes very close to the love-poets of the 16th and 17th centuries in England. In this respect, one is reminded of Herrick's lyric, which begins:

> Gather ye rosebuds while ye may,
> Old time is still a - flying.

and in which the English poet calls for the enjoyment of life while one still has youth and beauty.

But there is a basic difference between the love lyrics of 16th & 17th centuries in England, and the references to wine drinking and the sensual enjoyment of life in Khalili's poetry. The latter should be seen in its true perspective, as one more instance of a very long and old tradition of Sufi writing, dating back to the early Muslim mystics, such as Ibn Al-Faridh, and Jalaludin Balkhi Rumi (compatriot of Khalili). In their works, the Sufis expounded that the sole way of attaining God is through love and purification.

Life's harsh experiences: the injustice of man to man, oppression, war, poverty and death all occupy an important place in the verses of Professor Khalili. These, since time immemorial, have preoccupied the thoughts of poets and philosophers, thus illustrating the wisdom of the old French saying: "Plus ça change plus c'est la même chose"

Nevertheless, we do not feel any bitterness in Khalili's verses. Rather, we find that life's misfortunes, misery and even death, are accepted as they come, with the fortitude, courage, equanimity and self-confidence of a true believer in God.

Ala'uddin H. Aljubouri
Head, Department of Foreign Languages
Al-Mustansiriyah University
Baghdad. October, 1974

لست ارضى عن وردة حولهـا شو       ك ولا خمـــرة وراهــا صداع ؟

أيّ عمرٍ هـذا ولـو كان قـرنا       يعتريـه السـكوت والانقطاع ؟

Oh take away from me that rose with thorns!

Alas for that wine that gives headache!

Away with a life of a hundred years,

To be followed by a shameful moment of stillness.

دور افگنم آن غنچـــه کــه خاری دارد
فریاد ازان مي کـــه خمـاری دارد ،
بیــزار ز صـد ســال حیـاتي کز پي
یك لحظـــه سـكوت شرمبـاری دارد

كنت ِ تخفـين عن عيوني وجهــا      كربيع الحيــاة وردا وزهــــرا

وعلى البحـر قد رأيتـك غصنـا      البستـه الامـواج ماســـا ودرّا

Once I caught sight of your as a fair rose.

You looked like a pearl in the middle of the sea,

You were wont to hide one side of your face,

Yet, I was now able to see the whole of your bewitch-
ing figure!

دیدی که ترا چون گل زیبا دیــدم

ماننـــد گهــر در دل دریــا دیـــدم

تو گوشـــهٔ رخ ز من نهــان میکــردی

من شــــاخ گــل تــرا ســراپا دیـــدم

منهــل انت ام رســــول حبيبي ؟          بتّ تجري كدمعــي المحبـــوس

ـليس احلى من انبعــــائك تجــرى          في هدوء الصبــا ونــور الشموس

Oh spring, how sweetly do you flow!

Whose messenger are you? whence come you?

Like my tears, invisible to Man,

You flow gently , quietey , sweetly

ای چشمهء خوش چه جانفـزا می آیی ؟

پیغـامِ کــه ؟ داری زکجـا می آیی

مانند سـرشك من نهــان از مردم

آهسـته ونـرم وبی صـدا می آیی

لست اخشى الموت فالمـوت معيني        انــه في آخــر الامــر يقينــي

انــه أوصـــل أجـــدادى الى        مضجع ليس بـه غـير السكون

I face Death undaunted; it is my helpmate,

It affords me sustenance and consolation on my last
day;

It has accompanied my forefathers to their resting-
place,

This Death is my convenient mule!

از مرگ نترسم که مددگار من است

در روز پسین مونس و غمخوار من است

اجـداد مرا برده بســـر منزل شـــان

این مرکب خوشخرام رهوار من است

نحن تلك الثمــــــار فيهــا المرارا        ت سقطنا على ثرى الارض يومــا

ليس الا حريــــة للربيـــــع الـ        ـغض تحلــــو بها المرارة دوما

We are this bitter fruit, falling upon the earth.
Thus are we in the clutches of Time!
Oh spring of liberty! What else but your grace
Shall render this bitter fruit, sweet?

آن میـــوهء تلخیـــم کـــه ریزد بزمین

در پنجـهٔ ایـــام چنینیـــم چنـــین

جز فیض تو ای بهـــار آزادی چیست؟

کاین میوهء تلـــخ را نمایـــد شیـــرین

أيهـا الشَّيب قــد حكمت عليّ            بالرزايـــا والبـــؤس والآلام

كل ما قد يهون عنــدى ولكـــن            أنت أفقـدتني لـذيـذ الأنام


And you, hoary old age, though you have reduced me to
    a miserable wreck,
And condemned me to the harshness of Time,
Yet all this I can bear; but alas!
You have deprived me of the pleasure of sins!

پیری ! تو اگــر زار و تباهم کــردی

محکــوم جفــای سال و ماهــم کــردی

اینها همــه سهل است ولی حیف که تو

محروم ز لذت گناهـــــم کــردی ،

اذا صرت شيخا وارتجفت من العنا      فضاعف شربا من رحيق ومن خمر

فقـد لاعبتك الكائنات بمزحهـــا      فردّ عليهـا ضاحكا دون ان تدرى

When you are old, you will imbibe wine doubly,

You will hold your cup with a trembling hand;

Time has mocked and played tricks upon you,

Now, it is your turn to mock him, drinking with a
      laugh!

چون پیر شدی باده دو چندان می نوش!

پیمانهٔ می بدست لرزان می نوش!

بازیگر چرخ باتو بازیها کرد

بر بازی او بخند و خندان می نوش!

كنت طفلاً مدللاً حين اصغيت اللحن حلـو الى من بعيــد

واختفى الصوت اين ؟ كيف ؟ لماذا ؟         يا حنين الصبا واحلى العهود ؟

I was a child, slumbering in the crib of loving care;

Suddenly, some joyful tunes were heard in the distance;

Tunes that vanished as soon as I heard them,

Where, o where has the delights of youth disappeared?

طفلي بودم غنـــوده بر بســـتر نـاز

بر خاست ز دور نغمـــه های دمسـاز

تا گوش نهادم نـه صدا بود و نه ساز

ای شور جواني تو كجا رفتي بـــاز ؟

رب طــلاب شــهرة دون فضــل        غير تقتيـــل الناس والابريـــاء

صيَــروا العالــم الجميــل جحيما        وطلَــوْا وجهــه بلــون الدمــاء

Many a fame-seeker, an ignoble idler,

Has rendered the world a veritable hell;

Smeared the earth with the blood of the innocent,

So that so-and-so may become a celebrity!

شهرت طلبی بی هنری دونی چند
کردند جهان را بجهنّم ماننـد
صد بار زمین بخـون مردم تر شـد
تا نام فلان ابن فلان گشت بلنـد

اقبل الليـل' يا جميـل المحيّا !             فأت بالخمر مثل شمسك نـورا
كيف اغفو يا راحـة الروح فابحث            عن دواء يزيـدني تخــــديرا

O fair saqi[x] ! Where is your sparkling wine?
Where on this gloomy, dark night, is your sunlight?
Stories of life's mythe will not send me to slumber,
So, comforter, where is your soothing medicine?

---

x   Saqi: Cupbearer.

ای ساقی گلرخ ! می ناب تو کجاست ؟

در تیره شبِ غم افتاب تو کجاست ؟

زافسانـــهٔ روزگـار خـــوابم نبـــرد

ای راحت جان!داروی خواب تو کجاست؟

يا حفنة الطين ما هـذا الغرور وما          تبغي لنفسك من جـاه واعظـام

ما انت غير عظــام او خيوط دمٍ          فظاهــر خادع في باطــن دام

Oh handful of dust! Wherefore is your undue arrog-
ance?

Consider yourself for once, and contemplate your sig-
nificance;

A mere sackful of bones and two glasses of blood!

Therefore, what is your appearance, and what, your
reality?

ای مشتِ گل! این غرور بیجای تو چیست

یك بار بخود نگر كه معنای تو چیست

یك جعبهٔ استخوان دو پیمانهٔ خــون

پنهان تو چیست؟ آشكارای تو چیست؟

عقيلة الشخص قيـد لا يفارقـــه     كذاك حرقتـه في فرقـة الولـــد

والدهر يهزأ بالاشخاص قد غرسوا     بذر الهلاك ليلقوا مصرع الابــد

Many a man bound by the chains of matrimony,

Must perforce suffer the pangs of separation from his
     offspring;

That eternal cultivator, Time, will mock at him,

Who rejoices that the seed of death has been sown!

هر کس که به از دواج پا بند شـــود

معروض بــداغ ودرد فرزنــد شـــود

دهقان زمانـه بر کسـي مي خنـــدد

کز کِشتن تخم مرگ خرسند شـــود

مـا حياتي اذا خلت ْ من وجـــوه         فاتنـــات وســـكرة وشـــباب ،

مـا عـــدا قصـــة لحب عفيـف         هي عنـــدي تزين الف كتـــاب

Life is vain without a fair face,

Youth is futile without the purple wine;

And, in life, apart from the story if love,

All the letters you read or miss, are in vain!

بي روی نگـــار زندگاني عبث اسـت
بي بادهء گلفـــام جوانی عبث اسـت
در مکتب زندگي بجـــز قصهٔ عشـــق
هر حرف که خوانی ونخوانی عبث است

ان القوانين تحوى الف منفعـــة        وقــد تتيح ارتياحـا للملايـين

فاسلك مسالك اهل العشق حيث ترى        ان الـــذائذ في نقض القوانـين

The law may bring about a thousand advantages,

It may bring the people peace and relief,

But you have to follow the course of lovers,

To discover that its violation brings anothor joy!

قانون کـه هـزار سـود در بـر دارد

آسـایش خلـــق را میسّـــر دارد

در مسـلك عشق شو ! که آنجـا بینی

قانـون شـكني لذّت دیگـــر دارد

نحن في مسرح الحياة شـــــهود       والاعيب في يـــــــد الايتـــام

حيّرتنــا الحيــاة نرقص جهــلا       حين يأتي المجهــــول بالانغــام

We are the actors and the spectators in life's stage,

Perplexed in our work, bewildered at the riddle of the

      universe;

We are but small puppets in the hand of Time,

Dancing to the tunes of others!

بازیگــر و بــازی نگــر مَیـدانیــم
در کــار خـــود و کار جهــان حیرانیم
بازیچـــهٔ کوچکیـــم در دســت زمـان
هر ساز کـه دیگری کنـــد رقصانیم

والنجــم والشمس والأفلاك والقمر      يا من يرى ان هــذا الدهر خادمــه

تقتات من جسمك الخاوى فينذثر      اخشــى تراك جموع النمل خادمها

Oh proud man! Thinking that Time is at your service,

That the moon, the stars and the constellation your

    obedient servants;

I fear, rather, that it is those worms,

Feeding upon your corpse, that look upon you as their

    servant !

ای غرّه باینکـه دهـر فرمانبر تست
وین مـاه وسـتاره و فلک چاکر تست
ترسم که ترا چاکر خـود پندارنـــد
آن مورچگان که رزق شان پیکر تست

كم طُلِبنا عزّا وجاهـــا ومـــالا      وسعينا لشهرة ليس تُغني

واستَرحنا لمّا طوتنا المنايـا      بعد رَكضٍ وراءَ وَهمٍ وظَنّ

We have wasted a life-time looking for renown, glory
     and power;

Searching for fame we have become ill-famed;

But now thanks... thanks for being relieved of humil-
     iating competation,

For letting us rest everlastingly in this corner!

عمری پی جاه وعــزتو کام شـــدیم
عمری پی نام رفتــه بدنــام شـــدیم
صد شــکر کزان هرزه دوی آسـودیم
خفتیم درین گوشـــه وآرام شـــدیم

ثم قالـوا هــذه اسمى الفكـــــر          دَمَّروا الدنيا واؤدوا بالبشـــــــر

تحت اسـم الخير كم جاؤا بشــر !          ويحهــم كم انجبـــوا من فتــــــن

The Slaughter of Man is claimed to be "politics",
The destruction of the world is said to be "wisdom",
And under the guise of goodwill towards mankind,
They wrought havoc ; this is competence !

کشتند بشــر را که سیاست این است
کردنــد جهان تبــه که حکمت این است
در کســوت خیر خواهی نــوع بشــر
زادند چــه فتنه ها ؟ مهارت این است !

وما ملّنا اصطحابه      الكأسُ خلٌّ قديم

فالكرم باقٍ شبابه      فان كبِرنا وشِخْنا

Pour on wine! As yet, none has found it boring,

It is an old friend of whose company the heart never-
       tires;

We have grown old and youth has vanished,

Yet that fair daughter of Bacchus, never ages!

می ریز که کس زباده دلگیر نشد
یاری است کهن که دل ازاو سیر نشد
ما پیر شدیمو شد جوانی برباد
واین دختر عشوه باز رز پیر نشد

ملّة التوحيـد صـارت دوحــة          تســـتقي من منبـع لا ينضـب

وحّـدت اتباعهـا ... لكنهـم          كدجــاج حانـق يحتـرب ،

That Creed, advocating One God, is like a spreading
    tree,

Deriving life from the spring of one meadow;

Its adherents have preached the creed of unity unto
    the world;

Yet, like encaged hens, quarrel amongst themselves!

این ملّت توحید که از یک شــجرند

وز فیض بهاریک چمـــن جلــوه گرند

دادند بخلـــق درس یکرنگی وخـــود

چون مرغ قفس در شــکن یکدگرند

سيفـا ورمحـا ومكرا طـيه خُدَعِ' ؟      الى متى تتبـع الطغيـان منتضيـا

والحر يأباهما خلقـا ويرتفــع      فالبطش ذئب واصـل المكر ثعلبة

How long will you continue to hold sword and spear!

How long will you persist in treachery and fraud!

The one is a quality worthy of wolves, the other of
    foxes;

And once you are a man, you will be above both!

تا چنـــد پَي سنان و شمشير شـــوی ؟

تا چند پـی خدعـــه وتزویر شـــوی ؟

آن پیشهٔ گـرك باشد ، این از روباه

آدم چـو شوی زهردو دلگـیر شـــوی

سرى شموسا وأنجما ومجـــرة      يشــهد العارفون في الذرّة الصغـ

امّـا تمحــي بفعـــــل الـذرّة      ويرى فاقدو البصـائر فيهـــا

The philosopher sees a world in the heart of an atom,
He sees therein a sun, a moon and a constellation!
What blindness! In this world of us,
The scientist discrens the limbs and heads of the dead!!

عارف بدل ذرّه جهــــان مي بينـــد

آنجا مـه ومهـر و كهكشان مي بينـد

كوری بنگر ! كه چشم دانشور عصــر

پــا و ســر كشتگان دران مي بينـد

ايا جبـــلا فيم هـــذا الغرور ؟      وعجبك انــك تعلـو السحاب(١) ؟

فاني مـــع صغــــرى حـــرة      اطــير وانت ســـــجين التــراب


Oh mountain! high and mighty, reaching into the
     skies,

How you seem to be absorbed in self-admiration;

I am but a small bird, yet I am free to fly

From flower to flower, whilst you are in chains!

---

(١) الفراشة تخاطب الجبل

×   The butterfly says

ای کوه[۱] سرافراز فلك ساى بلنـــد !

تا چند به نخـوت و بلنـــدى خرسند؟

مـن طـایـر کـوچکـــم ولـي آزادم

من بر سر گل رقصم وتو پاى به بنــد

---

(۱)  پروانه به کوه میگوید .

لم نكـد نعـرف اسلوب الحيـاة      ونرى الأحيـا فاطبقنـا الشفاهـا

.واذا ما اشــتعلت ارواحنــا      فنيت كالشمع ، للغـير سناهـا

Soon as we've been immersed in the course of life,

We've opened our eyes, and closed our lips;

Just as we've lighted the torch of life,

We've burned like a candle, in the world of others!

تا مـا روش زمانــه آموختــه ایـم

بـا چشـم گشوده ولب دوختـه ایـم

تا مشـعل زندگی بر افروختـه ایـم

چون شمع به بزم دیگران سوخته ایـم

رُبَّ قومٍ تكالبـــوا كالــذئاب ،      وابتغــوا شــهرة بلا اســـــباب

غير قطـع الايدى وقتل البرايــا      والتعـالي في الناس كالاربـاب

Many a fame-hunter has conspired with his ilk,

Greedy for wealth, like a pack of wolves;

They have trampled thousands of heads and limbs un-
der foot,

So that they may arrogantly lift up their heads.

شهرت طلبی چنــد بهم ســاخته اند

چون گرگ گرسنه در جهان تاخته اند

کردند بزیر پا هزاران ســر و دسـت

تا گردن شــوم خــود برافراخته انــد

لا تنـيروا على ضريحي شموعـا ،    رحمــة بالفـراشـة الحوّامـــه

وأزيلـوا عنـه الريـاحـين رفقـا    بفـؤاد الجنـائني واهتمـامـــه

Oh do not place a lighted candle upon my grave,

Lest this should upset the innocent butterfly,

Or the gardener should experience the agony of fare-
well !

Oh do not place twigs and flowers upon my grave !

بــر تربت من شمع فروزان مگـــذار !

پـروانــهٔ زاررا پریشــان مگـــذار !

بــر خــاطر باغبـان منـه ! داغ جفـا

بــر تربت من سنبل و ریحـان مگذار !

قطــرة من دم تــراق بــلا حـــ٠٠٠٠ق كفص من خـاتم الغيب يلتقى

فاحـذر الدهرَ ان تهـــين يتيمـا       حيث يهتز العرش سخطا ورفقـا

Whenever a drop of blood falls upon the earth,

The ring of the heaven loses one of its stones;

Therefore beware! The sighs of an oppressed orphan,

Cause the edges of the mighty throne to breake down !

یك قطرهٔ خون كــه بر زمین می افتــد

از خـاتم آسـمـان نگـین می افتــد

هشـــدار ! كــه از آه یتیم مظلـــوم

بس كنگره كـز عرش برین می افتــد

ان قلبي في كـل حـال عمـادي      وهـو في عـالم الـوجـود إمامي

كلمـا ضقت من متاهـات عقلي      فلقلبي محبتـي واهتمـامي

My heart is, in all circumstances, my sustenance;

It is in this world of existence, my sovereign,

And when I am weary of the reign of reason.

God knows how grateful I am to my heart!

دل در همـه حـال تکیه گـاهست مـرا

در ملک وجـود پـاد شاهست مــرا

از فتنـهٔ عقـل چـون بجـان مي آیـم

ممنـون دلـم خـدا گـواهسـت مـرا

كـان غصن للـورد يضحـك امس    باسـمـاً للنسـرين والياسـمـين

حين لاحت في الافق نجمـة سحـر    حظهـا ضاحـك لعمـري الحزين

Yesterday the budding boughs were rejoicing in the
meadow,

Smiling at the hyacinth, the iris and the jasmin;

But all a sudden, the evening star appeared in the dis-
tant horizon;

Smiling complacently, mocking at my years!

دی شاخ شگوفه در چمن می خندید ،

بر سنبل و نسرین و سمن می خندید

از دور ستاره‌ٔ سحررا دیدم

بر بخت خود و بعمر من می خندید.

آيس كـالمـذاق في فـم مَيْـت      يَستوي الحـزن والسرور بقلـب

استـوى الامـر بين بُعدي وبيتي      واذا ناقتي عـلى الوحـل سـاخت

To the desperate, pleasure and sadness are all the same,

Sweetness and bitterness make no difference to the
     dead;

And should the feet of our camel sink deep in the mud,

What matters, if our home be near or far ?

بر خاطر مأيوس چــه ماتم چــه سرور

در ذائقه' مرده چه شيرين و چه شـور

چــون ناقه' سعي مــا فرو رفتـه بگل

سر منزل مقصود چه نزديك و چه دور

من الضنى والمآسي صاغني القدر     اوّاه من محنتي يا حظي العَثِر'

كشــمعــة في مهب الريح موقــدة     تذوى وتحرق حتى ينتهي العُمر'

Out of sickness and pain destiny has moulded me,

What, alas, has been my lot in life ?

Like to a burning candle, in the blowing wind,

I tremble, I burn, I die ............ alas !

از درد وال‍م سرشته تق‍دی‍رم حیف

از ساغر زندگي چه ح‍ظ گ‍یرم حیف

چون شمع که در معرض ب‍اد افروزند

م‍ي لرزم و م‍ي سوزم و م‍ي م‍یرم حیف

على شــفتي آهـــة تحـرق      وفي مهجتـي وتــر يفنـــرح'

فـان أغلقـوا منفـذاً للـرجـــاء      ففي المـوت نـافـذة' تفتَــح'

So long as a cry of pain lingers upon my lips,

There is still a string left in the heart's broken lyre,

If the gates of hope are shut befor me,

Yet there is death, like a crack in the wall !

تـا بـر لب من آه شـرربـاری هسـت

بر سـاز شکسته٬ دلم تـاری هسـت

درهـای امیـد را اگـر بـر بستنـد

تـا مـرگ بـود رخنهٔ دیـواری هست

أســفى أن تــرى الحيــاة نـدامــة      وعــذابـاً ومحنــة ودمــامــــه

فهــي أمــا تراك تحمــل ظلمـــا      أو ظلومـاً يخشــى الورى آثامـه

Alas ! Life has been a short but painful spell,

A tortured heart, an eye full of tears;

Either you bear, from day to day, the oppression of
tyrants,

Or you encumber the victim with more injustice.

افسوس كه زندگي دمي بــود و غمي

قلبي و شــكنجــه‌يي و چشــمي و نمي

يـا جــور ستمگـری كشيدن هر روز

يا خود بـه ستمكشي رساندن ستمي

وفــراقهــم مـوت بـلا أكفـــان      أصل' الهنــا في رفقــة الاحبــاب

فحيـاتنـا ومـاتنـا سيـــان      واذا غدا الاحباب في جوف الثّرى

The greatest joy is in the company of the loved ones,
The agony of death lies in being separated from them;
But since those, at last, are laid together in the dust,
What difference does it make whether we live or die?

سـرمـایهٔ عیش صحبت یـارانسـت
دشـواری مـرگ دوری ایشانسـت
چـون در دل خـاک نیز یاران جمعنـد
پس زندگي و مرگ بمـا یکسـانست

أملأ الكأسَ قد بدا قمـر الأفــق        فضـاءت كأسي وصارت شموسا

قمري مُؤنِسي مدى الدهر لـكن        قمر العلم صــار جرمـأ عبوسـا

Pour some wine ! The haloed moon has just appeared,

In its light, the wine-cup is glimmering like the sun;

What a big difference, the moon of love and that of science;

The one enjoys everlasting light; the other finds it a dark planet!

می ریز ! که ماه زد بگردون خــرگـــاه
گردید قدح چو مهر از پرتو مـــــــاه
فرق است میـــان مــه عشق و مــه علم
او نــور ازل بیند و این جــرم ســیـــاه

ومظهـر صيـغ من كبر وتزويق      ما نشوة النصر ما تاج وأوسمـة

مفـزّع الـروح من يتم وتمـزيق      أجلّ من فرحـة تنتاب قلب فتى

The joy of a pauper, finding a morsel of bread,

The delight of a needy lad, obtaining a garment,

Are surely equal to the raptures,

Felt by a victorious, conquering hero !

آن لقمـهٔ نــان کـه بینـوایـي یـابد
وان جـامـه کـه کـودك گدایـي یـابد
چون لـذت فتحي است کـه اقلیمي را
لشکـر شکنـي جهـان گشـایـي یـابد

وأنــا بــائس وأنت الــرحيـــم      «رب" يـا ذا الجــلال اني ضعيف

فابقني عنــك راضيــاً يا كريـم      كيف أرضيــك ذاك صعب علي"

Lord ! Thou art eternally wealthy, and I am but a
    mendicant,

Thou art omnipotent, glorious and I am weak,
    desperate;

To win thine approbation is no easy occupation,

To make me satisfied is infinitely easy !

یا رب تــو غنيّ مطلــق و من درویش

تو قــادر ذو الجـلال ومن زار و پریش

دشـوار بود که سازمت شـاد از خــود

سهل است مرا شاد نگهدار از خویش.

# المقَدِّمَة

هذه طاقةٌ عطرةٌ اقتطفَت من روضة رباعيّات الشاعر الانساني والمفكّر الأفغاني الكبير الاستاذ خليل الله خليلي ، سـفير أفغانستان في بغداد ، وتلبيةً لرغبة المغرمينَ بأدبهِ والمعجبينَ بشعرهِ طبعت ببغداد موطن الحضارة الاسلاميّة ومَوْئلها .

وببلاغة أديبٍ متضلّعٍ وشاعرٍ ملهم نقلها الى العربية نظماً سعادة السيّد أحمد حسين المروني سفير الجمهورية العربية اليمنيّة ببغداد

وقد قام الاستاذ الفاضل علاء الدين حمودي الجبوري رئيس قسـم اللغات الاجنبية في جامعة المستنصرية ببغـداد بترجمتهـا الى الانجليزيـة باسلوب نثري بديع .

بنام خداوند متعال

این مجموعه از رباعیات من که باز درد طنز مظلوم افغانستان و درد بار و درد ایران
طبع شد اخیراً با ترجمه عربی و انگلیسی در بغداد طبع گردیده  من از دوست بزرگوار
و محترم هموطن جناب سید ادریس علی شد.  سپاسگذار دارم که باز دیگر آنرا بدسترس من طبع
گذاشته اند.

جناب ادریس علی شد آثار گرانبهای  از افکار متفکرین اسلام تألیف و نشر
نموده ـ این آثار بشناساندن آن اندیشه های آسمانی مقام مولی عالی دارد
خصوص من در روزگار ما که ما دیات بر معنویات چیره شده و عقل سرگردان

فرزندان آدمی بهدایت نیخش بیشتر از هر وقت دیگر نیاز مندست .
حبیبی
۱۹/۳/۱۳۸۰

بخدمت عارف بزرگوار
دوست محترم جناب
ادریس علی شاه
تقدیم است

۱۹۷۷
خلیلی

# رُباعیات

## خلیل‌الله خلیلی